The Garden of Forgotten Echoes

In the stillness, whispers sigh,
Petals dance beneath the sky.
Memories bloom in gentle hues,
A tapestry of lost goodbyes.

Time drifts softly, shadows play,
Echos linger, night and day.
Silent paths where dreams once roamed,
The heart's soft garden, overgrown.

Moonlit beams on fragile leaves,
Stories woven in the eaves.
Each breath carries tales untold,
In this realm where time unfolds.

Step lightly 'mongst the sighing trees,
Embrace the hush upon the breeze.
Let the past weave through your chest,
In this garden, find your rest.

Flights through Shadows of the Past

In twilight's haze, the memories soar,
A canvas painted with dreams of yore.
Voices echo, familiar yet strange,
Through the corridors of time, they range.

Silent wings in dusky light,
Whispers beckon from the night.
Each shadow tells a tale anew,
Of paths once walked, of skies once blue.

The heart, a compass, seeks to know,
Where the rivers of time might flow.
In the dance of stars and sighs,
The past can teach, the present flies.

Beyond the veil, the stories blend,
A journey's start, a journey's end.
With open arms, I trace the night,
As shadows guide my fleeting flight.

Dusk's Illusionary Shores

Golden light fades soft and slow,
Whispers of night begin to grow.
Waves that sparkle in twilight's cloak,
Dreams unfurl like wisps of smoke.

Shadows dance upon the sand,
Mysteries weave, hand in hand.
The sea hums a lullaby,
As day bids the sun goodbye.

Footprints vanish with each tide,
Ebbing flows where secrets hide.
Stars above begin to gleam,
While the world melts into dream.

The Enchanted Dreamscape

In twilight's realm where shadows play,
Colors blend, then drift away.
Floating soft on whispered breeze,
Thoughts take root under ancient trees.

A symphony of sighing leaves,
Each note a tale the heart believes.
In the woods, where whispers dwell,
Magic weaves its subtle spell.

Luminous paths in silence glow,
Secrets only dreamers know.
Stars beckon from a velvet sky,
Daring hearts to soar and fly.

Fables of Forgotten Heroes

In quiet glades where ancients tread,
Stories linger, softly said.
Brave souls whispered to the trees,
Legends carried on the breeze.

With valor's flame they carved their way,
In battles fought, in skies of gray.
Though time may fade, their echoes stay,
Resilient hearts will find their play.

Beneath the stars, their tales resound,
In every shadow, truth is found.
Gone from sight, yet ever near,
These heroes live, their hopes sincere.

Pathways Overgrown with Time

Along the lane where wildflowers bloom,
Nature weaves from life's resume.
Twisting roots and brambles high,
Paths once clear now softly lie.

Memories linger in the air,
Whispers of journeys once laid bare.
Footfalls echo from the past,
In gardens wild, enchantments cast.

Each step taken, a story spun,
Underneath the watchful sun.
The heart finds peace in winding ground,
In overgrowth, a truth is found.

Enchanted Wastelands

Beneath the sky, a silence reigns,
Whispers of dreams, lost in the chains.
Gentle winds dance between the sands,
Where shadows play in distant lands.

Echoes of laughter, faint and low,
Crimson flowers begin to grow.
Among the ruins, secrets abide,
In the heart of stillness, worlds collide.

Moonlit nights with silver beams,
Awaken the magic, awaken the dreams.
A tapestry woven by nature's hand,
In enchanted wastelands, we take our stand.

Every step, a tale retold,
In a land of wonders, brave and bold.
Through the desolate, beauty we find,
In enchanted wastelands, hearts entwined.

The Lament of Withering Throne

Upon the hill, where shadows creep,
An ancient throne, a place to weep.
Crowned with thorns, memories frail,
Echoes of glory, now a veiled tale.

Once a beacon, bright and grand,
Now entangled in time's cruel hand.
The whispers of kings now fade away,
In the silence, the dreams decay.

Dusty banners, colors worn,
By the winds of fate, the crown is torn.
In the twilight, a sorrowful sigh,
For the withering throne, where legends die.

Yet beneath the sorrow, hope ignites,
In every heart, the strength unites.
From weary past, a future can grow,
As we rise from the ashes, the seeds we sow.

Tales from a Timeworn Trail

Winding paths through forest deep,
Where ancient secrets come to sleep.
Footsteps linger on the stones,
Listening close to whispered tones.

Echoes of travelers long since passed,
In stories woven, shadows cast.
Through rustling leaves and twilight's call,
In the soft glow, we hear them all.

Every bend holds a ghostly smile,
Recollections stretch for a mile.
With each step, the past unfurls,
In the dance of time, a world whirls.

From tales forgotten to dreams anew,
Through the timeworn trail, wanderers pursue.
In the heart of the journey, we find our way,
As life's vibrant colors blend and sway.

Memories Wrapped in Ivy

In the garden's heart, time stands still,
Wrapped in ivy, shadows fulfill.
Faded portraits, stories entwine,
In the hush of green, pasts combine.

Whispers of laughter, a gentle breeze,
Rustling leaves in the waking trees.
Among the blooms, recollections lie,
In the soft glow, where moments die.

Every petal holds a secret deep,
Soft echoes stirring from eternal sleep.
As ivy climbs, so do the dreams,
Through tangled vines, the memory gleams.

In this haven, we find our place,
Wrapped in ivy's warm embrace.
Through every season, love remains,
In the heart of the garden, a bond sustains.

Silent Gardens of Forgotten Hope

In the quiet grove, whispers dwell,
Where flowers bloom, and secrets tell.
Each petal soft, a tale once spun,
A tapestry of dreams undone.

Shadows linger, time stands still,
Echoes of laughter, a soothing thrill.
The sunbeams dance, in gentle sway,
As memories bloom in soft decay.

The Faded Colors of Memory

Once vibrant hues, now muted shades,
In the twilight glow, a bridge now fades.
Brushstrokes of time, on canvas worn,
Stories of love, and hearts forlorn.

Each glance recalls, a soft embrace,
In the quiet moments, find your place.
Though colors fade, the heart remains,
Cherished whispers in gentle refrains.

Etched in the Dust of Ages

Footprints linger on ancient stone,
Tales of the brave, now overgrown.
Whispers of time, in silence ring,
Legacies held by the winds of spring.

In every crack, a story lies,
Of wanderers, and starlit skies.
Dust speaks softly of battles fought,
Of victories gained, and lessons taught.

Owls and Shadows in a Moonlit Glade

In the hush of night, shadows creep,
As the owl calls from the depths of sleep.
Moonbeams weave through branches bare,
Whispers of magic fill the air.

Stars blink softly, a guiding light,
As nature's secrets unfold in flight.
Every rustle tells of tales unknown,
In the glade where wonder has grown.

Veils of Dust and Dreams

In the quiet hush of night,
Whispers dance in fading light.
Veils of dust and dreams entwine,
Secrets kept in fragile line.

Stars above, they softly gleam,
Guiding hearts that dare to dream.
Lost in thoughts, we float and sway,
Searching for the dawn of day.

Through the haze, the visions flow,
Carrying tales of long ago.
In the shadows, hopes reside,
Veils of dust, our dreams abide.

Time may fade and passion wane,
Yet the dreams will still remain.
Holding close what's dear and true,
Veils of dust, they shine anew.

Forgotten Paths in the Twilight

Beneath the arch of ancient trees,
Whispers stir with gentle breeze.
Forgotten paths in twilight glow,
Where the silent shadows flow.

Echoes linger, softly fade,
Memories in twilight laid.
Steps once bold, now cautious tread,
Following where dreams are led.

Fading light on trembling leaves,
Secrets linger, heart believes.
Paths once traveled now obscure,
Yet the soul finds ways to endure.

Twilight's charm, a sweet embrace,
Invites us to a hidden place.
Forgotten paths will lead us home,
In the twilight, we still roam.

Fragments of an Echoed Existence

In the corner of the mind,
Fragments lost, yet intertwined.
Echoed whispers, soft and low,
Stories of the life we know.

Time may bend and shadows stretch,
In twilight, memories etch.
Each fragment holds a tale to tell,
In this echoed, silent swell.

Moments linger, dance in air,
Haunting notes of love and care.
Life's mosaic, piece by piece,
In the echoes, find your peace.

Crimson skies, a fading hue,
Link the past to visions new.
Fragments of what once was real,
Echoed existence, hearts reveal.

Forgotten Paths in the Twilight

Beneath the arch of ancient trees,
Whispers stir with gentle breeze.
Forgotten paths in twilight glow,
Where the silent shadows flow.

Echoes linger, softly fade,
Memories in twilight laid.
Steps once bold, now cautious tread,
Following where dreams are led.

Fading light on trembling leaves,
Secrets linger, heart believes.
Paths once traveled now obscure,
Yet the soul finds ways to endure.

Twilight's charm, a sweet embrace,
Invites us to a hidden place.
Forgotten paths will lead us home,
In the twilight, we still roam.

Fragments of an Echoed Existence

In the corner of the mind,
Fragments lost, yet intertwined.
Echoed whispers, soft and low,
Stories of the life we know.

Time may bend and shadows stretch,
In twilight, memories etch.
Each fragment holds a tale to tell,
In this echoed, silent swell.

Moments linger, dance in air,
Haunting notes of love and care.
Life's mosaic, piece by piece,
In the echoes, find your peace.

Crimson skies, a fading hue,
Link the past to visions new.
Fragments of what once was real,
Echoed existence, hearts reveal.

Beneath the Weeping Walls

Beneath the weeping walls we stand,
Silent sorrow, a tearful land.
Ghosts of yesteryears arise,
Whispers trapped beneath gray skies.

Every crack holds tales of pain,
Rain-soaked dreams, our hearts remain.
Memories etched in every stone,
Beneath the walls, we are not alone.

Time moves on, yet shadows cling,
In the silence, echoes sing.
Beneath the weeping, life flows strong,
In the heart where we belong.

Hope emerges, breaking through,
New paths forged, with skies so blue.
Beneath the walls, we dream anew,
In the tears, we find what's true.

Whispers of an Abandoned Land

In fields where silence grows,
Wildflowers once danced free,
The wind now softly blows,
Carrying a memory.

Beneath the crumbling stone,
Echoes of laughter fade,
Ghosts of the seeds once sown,
In the twilight's shade.

Time weaves through the trees,
Tales of lives long past,
Nature hums a tune,
In shadows that will last.

Stars above begin to sigh,
As night embraces day,
In this land where dreams lie,
In whispers of decay.

Echoes in the Dust

Footprints lost in grains,
Stories left untold,
Among the ancient plains,
Whispers of the bold.

Time's embrace doth linger,
Clutching fragments tight,
Every breath a singer,
In the cloak of night.

The wind carries secrets,
Of lives entwined in fate,
Soft sputters and regrets,
Resting at the gate.

In shadows long and deep,
Memories intertwine,
Through silence they will seep,
In the dust, divine.

Shadows of a Distant Kingdom

Mountains rise like kings,
Veiled in misty dreams,
Where twilight softly clings,
To ancient flowing streams.

Castles worn by time,
Stones steeped in despair,
Echoes of a chime,
Drift in the cool air.

Lost in forgotten halls,
Faded tapestries,
A kingdom's silent calls,
Drowned by histories.

Beneath the emerald skies,
Whispers softly blend,
Where each starry guise,
Holds the tales to send.

Lost in the Veil of Time

Clocks stay frozen still,
As moments slip away,
In the valley's chill,
Shadows dance and sway.

Faded photographs,
Framed in golden years,
Echoes of our laughs,
Mixed with whispered fears.

The river's gentle flow,
Holds stories of the past,
Where memories still glow,
In hearts, they ever last.

Through the veil we roam,
Seeking what's concealed,
Yearning for a home,
In the time revealed.

Light through the Ashes

In the depths where shadows play,
Flickers of hope start to sway.
Each ember holds a whispered dream,
A gleam of light in sorrow's stream.

Through the dark, a path unfolds,
Stories of warmth, quietly told.
From the ruins, new life will arise,
As dawn brings forth the brightening skies.

In every burn, a lesson learned,
Through each scar, the heart has turned.
Cinders dance as spirits rise,
Feeding flames that never die.

So let the cold winds blow and sigh,
For beneath the ashes, dreams still lie.
With every breath, we pledge and fight,
To find our way, through the reclaiming light.

The Song of Silent Ruins

Echoes linger in the air,
Whispers of a past laid bare.
Stones stand guard with stories old,
In their silence, secrets unfold.

Once proud walls now gently weep,
Time has cradled them in sleep.
Nature weaves its hand so deft,
In the shadows, life is left.

Moss carpets where footsteps trod,
Cracks in stone where dreams once nod.
Breezes carry tales of yore,
An ancient song forevermore.

In the stillness, hearts will find,
The beauty left by humankind.
Each ruin sings a lullaby,
Of love and loss, beneath the sky.

Embers of an Ancient Hearth

In the glow of fading light,
Memories dance, hearts ignite.
Stories spun in warmth and cheer,
Echoes of those held most dear.

The scent of woodsmoke fills the air,
Whispers carried without a care.
Fires warmed by hands now gone,
Yet the hearth's glow lingers on.

Through the embers, spirits weave,
Tales of hope, dreams to believe.
In the quiet, a flickering spark,
Guides the way through the dark.

As twilight falls and shadows blend,
In this light, we find a friend.
An ancient warmth still holds its place,
In every heart, a timeless grace.

The Allure of Distant Horizons

Across the seas, the skies expand,
Whispers of journeys close at hand.
Veils of mist and dreams arise,
Call to souls with wandering eyes.

Mountains rise with quiet pride,
To secrets waiting deep inside.
The sun dips low, the stars ignite,
A tapestry of endless night.

With every breath, adventure calls,
In the echoes, wanderlust enthralls.
Each horizon, a tale unspun,
Underneath the watching sun.

So chase the dawn, where eagles soar,
To distant lands and unseen shores.
With open hearts, we set our sail,
For the allure of the unknown trail.

Secrets Beneath the Ruins

Whispers linger in the stones,
Silent tales of ancient homes.
Shadowed paths where echoes creep,
Guarding secrets still they keep.

Crumbled walls and ivy's grasp,
Time's embrace, a gentle clasp.
Faded murals tell the tale,
Of lives and dreams that softly pale.

Moonlight shines on what remains,
Lost within the tangled chains.
Footsteps shuffle, ghosts appear,
Carrying stories, drawing near.

Beneath the dust, the past awakes,
In whispered breaths, the silence breaks.
The ruins breathe a timeless sigh,
In every crack, a memory lies.

Echoing Silence of Yesterday

In the hush where shadows blend,
Time stands still, it does not end.
Footprints trace where dreams were sown,
In the comfort of the unknown.

Listen close, the silence speaks,
Of hidden paths and mystic peaks.
Faded laughter, a soft refrain,
Echoing whispers of joy and pain.

The heart remembers all it lost,
Every moment, every cost.
Yearning echoes in the air,
Softened sighs of sweet despair.

Through the night, the memories flow,
In silent depths, we come to know.
The past, like shadows, intertwine,
In reverence, we draw the line.

Reveries of a Faded Empire

Crimson banners, tales of old,
Whispers of glory, fortunes bold.
Once they danced on golden shores,
Now just linger, forgotten wars.

Ruined castles touch the skies,
Where dreams arose, now silence lies.
Stones that echo once proud cheers,
Now tell stories soaked in tears.

Chasing phantoms of the past,
Moments fleeting, shadows cast.
A faded realm where legends grew,
In quiet moments, they shine through.

Reflection deep, the heart will roam,
Through faded empires, seeking home.
History's breath, a gentle breeze,
In reveries, we find our peace.

Where Ghosts of Legends Wander

In twilight's glow, the legends walk,
In whispered tales, the shadows talk.
Echoes of glory, lost in time,
In every heartbeat, whispered rhyme.

Upon the hills where spirits play,
The ghostly echoes guide the way.
Through ancient trees, they weave and sway,
Telling stories of yesterday.

With every breath, the past returns,
Among the stars, their spirit burns.
In endless night, they dance and twine,
Chasing dreams across the line.

Here, the essence of hope remains,
In every joy, in every pain.
Where legends wander, time suspends,
In whispered dreams, the world transcends.

Tides of Memory in Haunted Waves

In shadows deep, the waters weep,
Forgotten whispers, secrets keep.
Ghostly echoes, tales unfold,
In haunted waves, the past retold.

Among the tides, lost dreams collide,
Silent stories, no place to hide.
Memories drift, a sea of sighs,
Under the moon, where time still flies.

Fleeting glimpses, like shells in sand,
Tracing footsteps, a guiding hand.
Ebb and flow of longing's pain,
In haunted waves, love's sweet refrain.

So sail along, your heart must dare,
Through tides of memory, find your prayer.
With every wave, let go, embrace,
The haunting pull of time and space.

Harsh Winds in the Labyrinth of Time

Beneath the sky, the storms arise,
Raging winds, relentless cries.
In tangled paths, we seek to find,
The fleeting moments that bind the mind.

Echoes linger, truths may bend,
Through labyrinths, we twist and wend.
Each gust a choice, each turn a chance,
In harsh winds, the heart's dance.

Shadows flicker, memories blend,
In the maze of hours, grief transcends.
Time's coarse breath, an endless race,
In the storm's heart, we find our place.

Through time's corridors, we wander far,
With every gust, seek your star.
Embrace the winds, both fierce and mild,
In the labyrinth of time, still a child.

Frayed Threads of Myth and Reality

In twilight's grasp, the stories fade,
Frayed threads of myth, the dreams we've made.
Reality bends, a paper thin line,
Between the heart's wish and the dark of time.

Legends whisper, shadows play,
Where truth and fiction gently sway.
In tangled yarns, our hopes entwine,
In frayed threads, a lifeline fine.

Each tale a spark, igniting the night,
Illusions dance, in flickering light.
With every stitch, we carve our fate,
In myth and reality, we all await.

So weave the cloth of dreams anew,
In timeless threads of vibrant hue.
Embrace the magic, both near and far,
In frayed threads, we find who we are.

Forgotten Colors on a Faded Canvas

Beneath the dust, the colors bleed,
Forgotten dreams lay bare their need.
On canvas worn, the strokes of time,
Each hue a story, each line a rhyme.

Memories linger, shades of past,
In silent whispers, their beauty cast.
Once vibrant laughs, now silent sighs,
In forgotten colors, the heart still tries.

Brushstrokes fade, yet hope remains,
In every corner, love still claims.
A palette rich with joy and pain,
On faded canvas, we dance again.

So gather up the hues of heart,
Revive the art where we once did start.
In every stroke, a breath of grace,
Forgotten colors find their place.

Ethereal Echoes of Old Worlds

Whispers of the past, they call,
In shadows where the ancients fall.
Starlit paths that glow in dreams,
Sailing on the moonlit beams.

Fleeting glimpses, soft and bright,
Guiding souls through endless night.
Memories in twilight's grace,
Carved in time, a hidden place.

Cascading through the ages lost,
In silence, hear the echo's cost.
Fragments of a tale untold,
Unraveling as stars unfold.

In these echoes, truth resides,
Where history and heart divides.
An endless dance, a timeless waltz,
In ethereal realms, the past exalts.

Relics of Celestial Governance

Glimmers in the cosmic dust,
Governed by the stars we trust.
Ancient rites of balance, spun,
As the music of the spheres runs.

Celestial bodies, in their dance,
Guardians of fate, they take their stance.
Constellations weave the laws,
Of night's embrace and morning's cause.

In the orbits, secrets hide,
Pulsing with the universe's tide.
The relics of a time once bright,
Carved in shadows, cloaked in light.

Echoes of a cosmic plan,
Binding the heart of every man.
In the stillness, truth ignites,
Relics glow in quiet nights.

Beneath the Canopy of Silence

Whispers linger in twilight's hue,
Beneath the canopies of dew.
Nature's breath in muted tones,
Cradles dreams in hushed groans.

The forest hums a tranquil song,
Where time seems to stretch long.
In shadows woven, secrets spun,
Where every leaf hides stories, done.

Footfalls tread on silent ground,
In reverence of peace profound.
Stars above blink soft replies,
In the stillness, the spirit flies.

With every heartbeat, silence speaks,
In layers deep, the wisdom seeks.
Beneath the boughs, a world anew,
Awaits the soul's embrace, so true.

Dreams Adrift on the Sea of Time

Waves of visions gently roll,
Carrying dreams toward the shoal.
Each ripple holds a whispered thought,
In the tides, our fate is caught.

Drifting far from shores of night,
Into the dawn, we chase the light.
Memories like shells, they gleam,
Stories woven in the stream.

Salted air and waves collide,
As time flows on, a joyous ride.
The horizon beckons, open wide,
Inviting every heart to glide.

On this sea, our dreams align,
In moments lost, a chance to shine.
Adrift we sail, in hopes sublime,
Forever dancing on the rhyme.

Sorrowful Echoes of the Unheard

Whispers in the shadowed hall,
Memories that never call.
A sigh that floats through endless night,
In silence lost, out of sight.

In corners dark, where feelings blend,
The time once shared, a bitter end.
Fading dreams like distant stars,
Haunted by their silent scars.

Each tear that falls, a story told,
Of laughter lost, of love grown cold.
Yet in the ache, a flicker stays,
For echoes linger, soft and gray.

A heart that beats, though bruised and worn,
Hopes wrapped tight in shadows' morn.
Still, in the depths, a whisper thrives,
Sorrowful echoes keep hope alive.

The Glimmering Dust of Old Yesterdays

Grains of time through fingers slip,
Whispers of the life we grip.
Moments captured, fading fast,
Shadows cast by ages past.

In glimmering dust, stories lie,
Hearts once danced beneath the sky.
Fragments scattered in the air,
Faded laughter, ghosts laid bare.

From old yesterdays, sweet refrain,
Echoes carried on the rain.
Each gentle drop, a memory,
Reminds us of what used to be.

Yet in this dust, a light remains,
Brightening the darkest pains.
We gather close, at dusk's embrace,
To find the warmth of time and space.

Notes in the Manuscript of Silence

In pages crisp of muted lines,
Unspoken words, like tangled vines.
Each note a breath that hangs in air,
Unheard melodies, a silent prayer.

With ink of tears, the verses flow,
In hidden depths, emotions grow.
A symphony of what's unsaid,
Haunts the heart and fills with dread.

Yet within this quiet tome,
Resides the seeds of dreams we've sown.
In silence bold, a truth unfurls,
The power lies in whispered worlds.

So let us cherish this still space,
Where thoughts can linger, hearts embrace.
For in the silence, beauty glows,
In notes that echo, love bestows.

Ghosts of What Might Have Been

Flickering lights in faded halls,
Echoes dance with whispered calls.
Paths untaken loom so clear,
Ghostly visions drawing near.

In corners where lost chances hide,
Regrets unfold, the heart's divide.
Dreams unspoken, hopes set free,
Float like whispers on the sea.

Threads of fate in shadows weave,
A tapestry of hearts that grieve.
Yet in the haunting, beauty lies,
In every tear, a new sunrise.

So let us honor those we miss,
And find the peace in what we wished.
For ghosts linger, lessons teach,
In every heart, they softly reach.

The Murmurs of Lost Wanderers

Whispers drift through shadowed trees,
Footsteps fade on ancient leaves.
Stories woven in twilight's breath,
Voices echo of love and death.

Eyes of wanderers greet the night,
Seeking solace, chasing light.
Fleeting dreams in twilight's grasp,
Moments linger, shadows clasp.

Lost in paths of memories drowned,
In every silence, tales abound.
The heart's compass, worn and frail,
Guides them through the unseen trail.

Underneath the starry skies,
Forgotten hopes and muted sighs.
The murmurs weave a tapestry,
Of wanderers who yearn to be free.

Ashen Paths through Time's Forest

Amidst the trees, the whispers twine,
Ashen paths where shadows align.
Time doth linger, caught in breath,
Dreams forgotten, dance with death.

Faint echoes of the past still call,
Through rustling leaves, they rise and fall.
Every step, a tale unfolds,
In haunted woods where time is cold.

The moonlight weaves through tangled brambles,
Illuminating days, now but scrambles.
Branches reach like hands in prayer,
Asking secrets they cannot bear.

Golden moments transformed to gray,
In a forest where shadows play.
Ashen paths like threads entwined,
Guide the lost, seeking peace of mind.

The Hollow Lament of Solitude

In empty rooms, the silence grows,
Whispers fade where no one goes.
Shadows dance upon the floor,
With memories locked behind a door.

A heart beats softly in the dark,
Echoing hopes that left their mark.
Each sigh a story left untold,
In the chilling arms of the cold.

Time drips slowly, like melting wax,
Beneath the weight of all that lacks.
The hollow cries of what once was,
A broken tune, a fractured pause.

Yet in the stillness, strength is found,
In solitude's embrace, profound.
The lament sings through endless nights,
An anthem of unseen fights.

The Faint Glow of the Inexplicable

In the stillness of the night,
A flicker glows, both ghost and light.
Mysteries dance in shadows' sway,
Polishing truths that drift away.

Whispers of the stars above,
Carry secrets wrapped in love.
Ethereal visions softly gleam,
In flickering traces of a dream.

The heart leaps at the unseen veil,
Unraveling threads of a timeless tale.
Every sigh, a spark ignites,
Guiding seekers through the blights.

In the distance, a call persists,
A faint glow through the morning mists.
Though inexplicable paths may wend,
Hope's tender light will always mend.

The Beauty of What Has Gone

In the dusk of fading light,
Memories linger, soft and bright.
Whispers of a time once known,
In shadows, the beauty has grown.

Leaves that danced in autumn's breeze,
Echoes carried through the trees.
Moments cherished, now they fade,
Yet in hearts, their warmth is laid.

Glimmers of a laughter shared,
Caught in threads of love declared.
Though the past is far away,
In our souls, it will always stay.

In the silence, hear the call,
Of stories woven, one and all.
The beauty of what has been,
Lives on in the spaces within.

Starlight Failed to Return

In the night, the stars are few,
Flickers lost in shades of blue.
The cosmos sighs a muted tune,
As shadows hide the pale moon.

Whispers drift on a midnight air,
Promises made, a vacant stare.
Each twinkle once bright and bold,
Now draped in a shroud of cold.

Time erodes what once was clear,
Wishes flying, lost from here.
The starlight fades, a restless dance,
Leaving hopes in a silent trance.

Yet in the void, a spark ignites,
A yearning for those distant lights.
Though starlight failed to return,
In our hearts, its glow will burn.

Pages Torn from Guardian Books

History rests on tattered sheets,
Stories whispered in covert beats.
Pages worn, their truth outflows,
Guardian tales that nobody knows.

Time's fingers pull, tearing seams,
Rewriting fates, shattering dreams.
Fragments scatter, lost to the winds,
Each page a tale that fate rescinds.

Echoes linger, voices blend,
In the silence, the stories mend.
Guardians watch from shadows cast,
Enshrined in the silence of the past.

Yet even torn, those pages gleam,
Holding the strength of every dream.
Guardian hearts in whispers speak,
As the lost find a path to seek.

The Remnants of Fallen Kings

Broken crowns on the dusty ground,
Echoes of power once profound.
Fallen banners weave through the breeze,
Tales of glory brought to their knees.

Ruins speak in solemn tones,
Forgotten thrones of silent bones.
Shadows dance where kings once stood,
In the remnants, a story brewed.

Reverence hangs in the air,
As whispers speak of pride and care.
Each crumbling stone, a memory sung,
The legacy of what was once begun.

In the twilight, their spirits breathe,
The lessons learned, they still bequeath.
For those who rose, and those who fell,
In the remnants, their stories dwell.

The Remains of Dusk's Embrace

The sky darkens, hues of gold,
Whispers of twilight, stories untold.
Shadows stretch as day bids adieu,
Echoes linger in the fading blue.

Ghostly silhouettes dance on the ground,
Lost in the silence, a peace profound.
Stars awaken, glimmering bright,
Holding the secrets of the night.

In the stillness, memories weave,
Tales of heartache and tales of leave.
As the moon rises, dreams ignite,
In the remains of dusk's embrace, so light.

Time pauses, life's dance slows down,
Nature cloaked in a soft, dark gown.
Beneath the heavens, we find our place,
In the gentle hold of dusk's embrace.

Haunting Melodies of Solitude

In the silence, a soft refrain,
Melancholy sings of joy and pain.
Lonely echoes drift through the air,
Haunting melodies, fraught with despair.

A lonesome tune, a bittersweet cry,
Resonates softly, as shadows comply.
Each note a story left to unfold,
In the heart of the lonely, brave and bold.

Whispers of longing, soft as a sigh,
In the depths of solitude, dreams often die.
Yet in the stillness, strength is found,
In the haunting melodies, deeply profound.

The night carries songs, frail yet strong,
Reminding the weary they still belong.
In each solitary moment, we find a way,
To dance with the shadows, to feel, to sway.

The Unseen Gallery of Time

Canvas of moments, painted with care,
Frameless, untouched, hanging in air.
Brushstrokes of laughter, tears, and grace,
The unseen gallery, a sacred space.

Each tick a heartbeat, each tock a sigh,
Displaying the life that passes us by.
Memories linger, a haunting refrain,
In this gallery, joy mingles with pain.

Time's gentle hands sculpt the unknown,
Curating whispers of seeds we've sown.
Portraits of love and hearts left behind,
In the unseen gallery, truths intertwined.

As we wander through shadows and light,
Each glance reveals what's hidden from sight.
In the fabric of hours, we seek to find,
The stories of souls, forever entwined.

Traces of a Once-Alive World

In the ruins of time, shadows lay bare,
Faint echoes of laughter fill the air.
Ghosts of the past in the places we roam,
Whispering stories of a long-lost home.

Decayed walls reveal what's faded away,
Memories linger where children would play.
The songs of the streets, now silent and cold,
Hold traces of warmth, of lives once bold.

Nature reclaims what time has forsaken,
Flowers bloom where hearts were awakened.
Every fragment of life, a story retold,
In the remnants of dreams, both vibrant and old.

We wander these paths, both wistful and sad,
Reflecting on beauty, the good and the bad.
In the traces of a once-alive world,
Hope intermingles with the memories swirled.

Eclipsed by a Whispering Night

In shadows deep the silence sighs,
Stars twinkle dimly in the sky.
Moonlight dances on the ground,
Lost in dreams, no footsteps sound.

A chill winds through the ancient trees,
Whispers carried on the breeze.
Souls long gone now softly speak,
In the dark, it's peace they seek.

The night unfolds its velvet cloak,
As secrets mingle, words provoke.
What once was bright now dims away,
Beneath the watchful skies of gray.

Eclipsed by thoughts we dare not share,
Hope flickers low, a tender flare.
Yet in this stillness, truth takes flight,
Embraced gently by the night.

Starlit Visions of What Once Was

Faded echoes of laughter ring,
In the hush where fireflies sing.
Memories linger, soft and sweet,
Dancing where past and present meet.

Each star above holds tales untold,
Whispers of love, both young and old.
Glimmers of joy, shadows of pain,
In the night's embrace, all remain.

Time paints the skies with silver light,
Remnants of dreams lost to the night.
Yet starlit visions blaze anew,
Binding the old with threads of blue.

In endless skies the stories weave,
In every twinkle, hearts believe.
From dusk till dawn, the cycle flows,
In starlit realms, the spirit grows.

The Sorrowful Song of Lost Souls

In the shadows where spirits weep,
Echoes of sorrow gently creep.
A melody of longing sighs,
In the night, the lost souls rise.

Each note a tale of dreams denied,
Adrift in time, with nowhere to hide.
Whispers trace the path of pain,
A haunting song that still remains.

Through the mist, their voices blend,
A mournful hymn that will not end.
Threads of sadness, woven tight,
In the darkness, they seek the light.

Yet amid the grief, hope dares to glow,
For love persists, though spirits go.
In every heart, their song will dwell,
A timeless echo, a bittersweet bell.

Secrets in the Cracks of Time

In the corners where shadows lie,
Time holds secrets that whisper nigh.
Cracks in the walls of yesterday,
Hide fragments of what slipped away.

Dusty volumes of stories old,
Tales of warmth, of hearts consoled.
Silent pages beckon out,
Revealing what life's about.

Each moment etched in fleeting grace,
Lost in a dream, a fleeting trace.
Yet in those cracks, we find the light,
Glimmers of truth that banish night.

So pause to listen, let it unfold,
The secrets of life, both cruel and bold.
In every crack, a memory lies,
An echo of love that never dies.

Footfalls among the Whispering Pines

Beneath the boughs, the silence reigns,
Where nature sings in joyful strains.
Footfalls linger, whispers low,
In the heart of pines, where dreams do flow.

Moonlight dances on the ground,
A magic spell that wraps around.
In every shadow, secrets hide,
Among the trees, where spirits glide.

The breeze carries tales untold,
Of nights beneath the stars so bold.
Each rustle, each sigh, a gentle tease,
In whispered tones, the pines appease.

So here I wander, lost in thought,
In the solace that this place has brought.
Among the whispering pines, I find,
A refuge sweet, to ease my mind.

Unremembered Faces of Forgotten Places

In corners of the mind, they dwell,
Faint echoes of a distant bell.
Unremembered faces, lost in time,
Whispers in the wind, a silent rhyme.

Forgotten places, shadows cast,
Memories ebb, like a fading past.
Once vibrant scenes now dimmed by gray,
Yet in the heart, they find their way.

Faces flicker in the candle's glow,
Stories woven, threads to sow.
In the silence, laughter once rang,
Now echoes softly, a ghostly clang.

Though time may steal, and space may fade,
In dreams they come, unafraid.
These fleeting glimpses, a haunting grace,
Unremembered faces, lost in place.

The Lost Verses of Yesterday

In the pages of the past, they lay,
Words forgotten, drifting away.
The lost verses of a time long gone,
Echoes of voices in a haunting song.

Each line a memory, rich and deep,
In the shadows, their secrets keep.
A dance of ink on weathered sheets,
In the still of night, the heartbeat beats.

With every sigh, a story fades,
In silence, the beauty wades.
Yet in the heart, a flicker glows,
The lost verses whisper, as the spirit knows.

So gather them close, these words of old,
A tapestry of dreams retold.
In the light of dawn, let them arise,
The lost verses, beneath vast skies.

Light Amidst the Shadows of Oblivion

In the depth of night, a glimmer shines,
A beacon bright, where hope entwines.
Light amidst the shadows, softly glows,
Guiding the way, where darkness flows.

Through the veil of silence, it breaks free,
A whispered word, a sacred plea.
In the heart of shadows, calm and still,
The light persists, a vibrant will.

Each flicker dances, a tale to share,
In the quiet corners, it lingers there.
A flicker of faith, amidst the gloom,
Banishing fears, dispelling doom.

For in the shadows, light takes its stand,
A gentle touch, a guiding hand.
So let it rise, this flame so bright,
A promise of dawn, beyond the night.

Whispers from the Edge of Forgotten

In shadows where the lost reside,
Soft murmurs linger, secrets hide.
Echoes brush against the night,
Carried on winds, a fleeting flight.

Faded memories dance around,
In silence, the past might be found.
Ghostly figures beckon near,
Whispers of what we held dear.

Stars shimmer with tales untold,
Of dreams once bright, now dimmed and cold.
On the edge, time stands still,
Chasing echoes against our will.

The moon shines down with silver grace,
Illuminating this sacred place.
In twilight's grasp, the lost convene,
To share the tales that might have been.

Elysium of the Lost and Longing

In fields where shadows softly play,
The lost dreams yearn for the light of day.
Whispers of hope in the breeze,
Caress the heart like gentle trees.

Moonlit nights bring solace sweet,
Where longing hearts and silence meet.
In the quiet, we find our way,
Through memories that softly sway.

Elysium calls from beyond the mist,
Where sorrow fades, and joy persists.
A fleeting glimpse of what we seek,
In each sigh, in each heartbeat.

We wander through this sacred space,
Touching the void, yearning to embrace.
Among the lost, we find our song,
In the beauty where we all belong.

Echoes of a Lost Paradise

In gardens where the silence reigns,
The whispers of time fill the plains.
Petals fall like forgotten dreams,
Echoes dance in soft moon beams.

The brook babbles tales of old,
Of hearts entwined and love so bold.
Each ripple sings a haunting tune,
Lost paradise, gone too soon.

The shadows stretch, as day turns night,
In dreams, the past ignites the light.
We search for places once known well,
In memories where we used to dwell.

Yet echoes linger, soft and clear,
A reminder of what once was dear.
In this twilight, we roam and sigh,
In a paradise we're left to cry.

Whispers in the Twilight Forest

In twilight's grip, the forest whispers,
Among the trees where the soft light glisters.
Shadows play on the mossy ground,
Secrets of the wild abound.

Crickets sing in harmony,
With winds that tell of memory.
A rustle here, a gentle call,
As twilight weaves its magic thrall.

Through ancient woods, our spirits roam,
In nature's arms, we find our home.
Each step echoes a tale once lost,
In the silence, we embrace the frost.

Embers fade as the stars appear,
In this sacred space, we draw near.
With whispers soft and love profound,
In twilight's hold, we are unbound.

Chronicles of the Unseen

In shadows deep, they tread so light,
A world untouched by day or night.
Whispers stir in silence rare,
Secrets kept, they linger there.

Through veils of mist, their stories weave,
In every heart, they take their leave.
Faint echoes softly call their name,
In dreams of dusk, they spark the flame.

Lost in time, where moments flow,
In hidden paths, the ancients go.
A tale unfolds, yet left unseen,
In night's embrace, they dwell between.

So listen close, heed the sighs,
For unseen worlds wear many guise.
Each word a thread, each breath a clue,
Chronicles fade, but truth rings true.

Candlelight Flickers in the Void

A candle's glow in darkness wide,
Flickers swift, where secrets hide.
Dim reflections dance on the wall,
In silence deep, they heed the call.

Faint shadows play, they twist and bend,
A soft embrace, where dreams descend.
In every flicker, hope ignites,
A beacon bright in longest nights.

The flame whispers of tales untold,
Of brave hearts and treasures bold.
Yet in the void, it softly weeps,
For long-lost souls that silence keeps.

So let it burn, this light so small,
In darkest times, it conquers all.
With every breath, it leads the way,
Candlelight flickers, come what may.

The Song of Ancient Echoes

In valleys deep, where echoes play,
Ancient songs drift far away.
Melodies of time long past,
Whispers of the world amassed.

Each note a thread, each chord a tie,
Binding souls who lived and die.
Tales of love, of loss, of fears,
Resounding still through countless years.

In twilight's glow, the echoes rise,
Carried forth on gentle sighs.
A harmony of life and fate,
In every sound, we contemplate.

So listen close, let spirits soar,
To songs of old, forever more.
In every heart, they find their place,
The song of echoes, woven grace.

Windswept Whispers of Old Tales

The wind carries tales from afar,
Of wandering hearts and dreams ajar.
In every gust, a story spins,
Of loss and love, where hope begins.

Through rustling leaves and mountain high,
Whispers dance beneath the sky.
Faint echoes of what used to be,
In every sigh, sweet memory.

The ages weave with threads of grace,
As time unveils each hidden space.
In windswept nights, the voices call,
Tales of glory and those who fall.

So let the whispers guide your way,
In every breeze, let dreams convey.
For old tales live, in every breath,
In windswept whispers, life meets death.

Ghostly Footprints on Forgotten Paths

In the silence of the night,
Whispers dance with the breeze,
Lost souls tread on ancient trails,
Leaving traces that never cease.

Moonlight casts a silver glow,
Shadows stretch and intertwine,
Echoes of lives long departed,
Mark the journey's thin design.

Footsteps faded, stories told,
Through the woods, they gently roam,
Carrying secrets of the past,
Searching for a place called home.

In the mist where silence reigns,
Ghostly forms may haunt the way,
Yet the footprints softly linger,
Waiting for the break of day.

Sunlight through the Ruined Arches

Golden rays pierce through the stone,
Illuminating tales once grand,
Whispers of a time long past,
In the sunlight's gentle hand.

Arches stand with stories deep,
Crumbled walls that time forgot,
Memories in each shadow play,
Of battles fought and love's true knot.

Nature intertwines with the old,
Vines embrace the remnants fine,
Sunshine brings a warmth so bold,
Life returns, the ruins shine.

Each beam of light a soft caress,
Awakening the heart's own spark,
Reminding us of beauty's grace,
In the depths of the faded dark.

The Forgotten Path of Wanderers

Beneath the canopy of leaves,
A path lies shrouded in the mist,
Footsteps lost in nature's weave,
Where whispers of the past persist.

Wanderers tread with heavy hearts,
Dreams carried in weary souls,
Searching for a place to start,
As time's gentle river rolls.

Each bend reveals a tale unknown,
With every leaf, a story shared,
Of love, of loss, of seeds once sown,
In the silence, they are bared.

Yet under the stars, hope beckons,
Guiding those who dare to roam,
Through the night, the spirit reckons,
Finding in the dark their home.

The Melancholy of Vanished Dreams

In the twilight of lost hopes,
Shadows gather, silence sighs,
Echoes linger, time elopes,
As the heart in stillness cries.

Wishes woven in twilight's seam,
Faded like whispers on the wave,
Memories drift, like a broken dream,
In the quiet, their beauty braves.

Stars above wink with regret,
For the dreams that slipped away,
Each twinkle a silent fret,
In the night, they long to stay.

Yet from the ashes, embers glow,
A reminder of what once was bright,
In every sorrow, there's room to grow,
For hope is born in the heart's soft light.

The Silence of Hidden Valleys

In valleys where whispers fade,
The secrets of the earth are laid.
Beneath the canopy of green,
A world untouched, serene.

The murmurs of the winds do weave,
In shadows where the lost believe.
Time lingers in the sacred groves,
Among the paths that memory roves.

A dance of leaves upon the ground,
In silence, ancient echoes sound.
Here nature's breath is felt the most,
A haven where the heart may coast.

O hidden valleys, deep and wide,
With you, the restless spirits bide.
In hushed repose, the dreams take flight,
Within your arms, the stars ignite.

Ghost Lights in the Misty Hollow

In the hollow where the shadows play,
Bright ghost lights beckon night and day.
They weave through trees like whispered sighs,
A fleeting glimpse that mystifies.

Soft echoes float on the midnight air,
Ghostly figures, subtle and rare.
They dance on paths of silver dew,
Enticing hearts to wander through.

Misty shrouds embrace the land,
As flickering lights take a stand.
Lost souls wander, drawn to the call,
Of luminescence, enchanting all.

Through the depths of fear and fright,
In the hollow, they find light.
For in the dark, we learn to see,
The beauty of the mystery.

Legends of the Steel-Bound Wood

In steel-bound woods where legends lie,
Trees whisper tales beneath the sky.
Knotted branches, ancient and wise,
Guard the secrets that never die.

Footsteps echo on soft decay,
In the heart of the forest's fray.
Here knights and shadows once stood tall,
A realm of wonder, embracing all.

Beneath the moss, the stories sleep,
Of brave souls and promises to keep.
With every breeze, a voice calls near,
A reminder that magic is here.

In the glow of dusk, they rise anew,
Legends reborn as the night breaks through.
In steel-bound woods, history's thread,
Weaves through hearts long after they're dead.

The Magic of Yesteryears

In twilight's glow, the past appears,
Whispers wrap like silken shears.
Memories dance in shadows light,
The magic of yesteryears ignites.

Old photographs with faded hues,
Tell tales of life in vibrant views.
Each glance a portal, a fleeting glance,
A chance to meet fate's curious dance.

With laughter echoing through the halls,
Time unfurls, as the spirit calls.
In every corner, a story dwells,
Of love and loss, and all it tells.

The magic lingers, forever clear,
In the heartbeats of those held dear.
Embrace the past, let it abide,
For yesteryears bring warmth inside.

The Abyss of Unremembered Tales

In shadows deep, where whispers fade,
The tales of old begin to wade.
Fragments of voices call and creep,
Into the night, where secrets sleep.

Forgotten dreams on twisted paths,
Echo in silence, the mind's aftermath.
Each story lost, a flickering flame,
In the abyss, they call my name.

Veil of mist, shrouded in pain,
Memories lost, like drops of rain.
This hollow void, a canvas bare,
A haunting dance of loss and despair.

Yet in this realm, hope softly gleams,
For unremembered tales weave new dreams.
With heart in hand, I'll search anew,
Seek the light where shadows grew.

Timeless Treasures in Dusty Corners

In corners dim, where dust resides,
Lie treasures lost, where time abides.
Old photographs, their faces aged,
Whispering tales, as life engaged.

Books with spines like weathered skin,
Holding secrets of what has been.
Page by page, the stories flow,
In dusty corners, memories glow.

A rusty key, a forgotten chest,
Each item holds a tale expressed.
Life once lived in curio's heart,
In timeless treasures, we find our part.

With every touch, the past awakes,
In gentle hands, the silence breaks.
From dusty nooks, our history sings,
Of timeless treasures and fragile things.

Fragments of a Tattered Map

A tattered map with faded lines,
Holds stories lost, of distant times.
Each torn edge a path unknown,
Leading to places we've never grown.

In corners marked with faded ink,
Lies a world we've yet to think.
X marks the spot where wishes hide,
Fragments whisper of tides and pride.

These remnants speak of journeys past,
Of fleeting moments, gone too fast.
Paths intersect where dreams collide,
With fragments guiding what's inside.

So onward I tread, with the map in hand,
Searching for treasures across the land.
Each fragment leads to a spark anew,
On this journey, I'll find my truth.

Beneath the Weight of Lost Histories

Beneath the weight of shadows cast,
Lie stories buried, long since passed.
Echoes linger, a silent plea,
For lost histories to set them free.

In every stone, a tale resides,
Of those who came and dared to hide.
A tapestry woven, thread by thread,
From lives once lived, now echoing dead.

The clock ticks on, but time stands still,
As memories rise like a heavy chill.
Under the weight of what was lost,
We find the path, no matter the cost.

Yet in this search for what's now gone,
We gather strength to carry on.
Beneath the weight, we find our voice,
In lost histories, we make our choice.

Haunting Melodies of the Past

In shadows dance the notes of old,
Whispers of dreams that once were bold.
Echoes linger in moonlit air,
Softly hum the tales we share.

Each chord a memory intertwined,
Fading softly, yet unconfined.
They weave through time, a gentle sway,
Guiding hearts that long to stay.

The past sings sweetly, bittersweet,
In every pulse, our lives repeat.
Fleeting moments in twilight's grace,
Forever held in time's embrace.

Let the haunting melodies play on,
A symphony of love not gone.
In every heart, a song will bind,
The echoes of a wandering mind.

The Veil of Time's Embrace

A shroud of mist, a veil so thin,
Hides the stories we hold within.
Time whispers secrets through the air,
In every glance, a lingering stare.

The past and future intertwine,
A tapestry, both yours and mine.
Moments captured in silent grace,
Fleeting visions in time's embrace.

A heartbeat echoes, soft and low,
In shadows cast by long ago.
Each step we take, a thread we trace,
Through the veils that time can't erase.

Awakened dreams in twilight's hue,
Reveal the paths we all once knew.
In night's embrace, we find our place,
A dance of souls, with silent space.

Memories of a Sunken City

Beneath the waves, where silence dwells,
A city sleeps, its ancient bells.
Stones weathered by the tides of time,
Whisper tales in the ocean's rhyme.

Ghostly ruins in the deep blue,
Echoes of laughter, soft and true.
Lost in currents, shadows roam,
Seeking solace, far from home.

Coral gardens hide the past,
In sparkling depths, forgotten cast.
Each fragment tells a story grand,
Of love and loss in a distant land.

With every wave that kisses shore,
The sunken city breathes once more.
Memories rise like rising tides,
In the heart of the sea where time resides.

Crumbling Stones of a Distant Age

In fields where shadows softly creep,
Stand crumbling stones, their tales run deep.
Whispers of warriors long since passed,
Echo in the winds that forever last.

Nature weaves through cracks and seams,
Filling space with half-remembered dreams.
The weight of history, strong yet frail,
Marks the path of every tale.

Moss-covered walls hold secrets tight,
Beneath the stars, they claim their night.
Each fragment speaks, a silent sage,
Of glory and grief from a distant age.

In every stone, a life persists,
The warmth of laughter, the chill of mists.
Crumbling stones in twilight's glow,
Remind us all of what we know.

Remnants of Celestial Gleam

In a sky where stars once danced,
Light whispers secrets lost in trance.
Fragments of dreams, they weave and sway,
Guiding the night, they softly play.

Moonbeams trace the paths of old,
Tales of love in silver unfold.
Ancient echoes in twilight's hum,
A symphony of what's to come.

Faded memories, soft and bright,
Cradle the heart in gentle light.
Time drifts on, yet they remain,
Remnants of joy mixed with pain.

Upon the breeze, a sigh of peace,
Celestial songs that never cease.
As shadows dance in twilight's beam,
We find solace in the gleam.

Chronicles of the Disappeared

In forgotten corners, shadows creep,
Whispered stories aim to keep.
Faces fade like mist at dawn,
Echoes linger, memories drawn.

Worn pages tell of battles lost,
Dreams now buried, counting cost.
The heart recalls what eyes can't see,
Chronicles wrapped in mystery.

Lost whispers float on silent air,
Tracing footsteps, unaware.
In every sigh, a tale resides,
Of those who fled, their hopes and hides.

Yet in the silence, truths abound,
In every loss, new life is found.
We weave their threads in the tapestry,
Chronicles of lost history.

Twilight Gardens of Yore

In the stillness where the twilight breathes,
Gardens hum with ancient leaves.
Petals fall like whispered dreams,
Caught in the glow of fading beams.

Once, laughter danced upon the air,
Now echoes linger; a gentle prayer.
Sunset's kiss paints shadows long,
In this haven, where we belong.

Time slows down, the moment sways,
Nature's canvas, a soft display.
Each flower, a story, a memory sown,
In twilight's embrace, we're never alone.

Entwined with magic, every glance,
In twilight gardens, we find our chance.
To wander through dreams beneath the trees,
And cherish the night on a gentle breeze.

Lost Legends in the Mist

Fog descends on hills of lore,
Hiding tales from days before.
In shadows thick, the past conceals,
Secrets whispered, time reveals.

Voices echo through the haze,
Murmurs of forgotten ways.
Legends wander, lost yet found,
In the silence, truths abound.

Each step taken, a bridge to the past,
Stories linger, shadows cast.
In the mist, we seek and yearn,
For tales of old, we slowly learn.

With every breath, we weave anew,
The fabric of history cloaked in blue.
Lost legends call through the shifting veil,
In the heart of the mist, the tales prevail.

Shadows Beneath the Ancient Towers

In twilight's grasp, the shadows creep,
Where ancient stones their secrets keep.
The wind whispers tales of yore,
Echoes fading evermore.

Moss-covered paths, a silent guide,
Beneath the towers, hopes reside.
Forgotten dreams, they softly sigh,
As stars awaken in the sky.

The moonlight dances on the walls,
While time itself no longer calls.
In silence deep, the memories lay,
Awaiting night to shape the day.

Secrets of the Silent Grove

Beneath the boughs, where silence reigns,
The whispers of the past still stain.
With every step, the soft earth sighs,
A breath from long-forgotten skies.

The leaves conceal old tales untold,
As shadows move, so brave, so bold.
The stars peek through, like watchful eyes,
Tracing paths where magic lies.

A brook flows gently in the night,
Guiding dreams toward hidden light.
In quiet grace, the grove unfolds,
Its secrets kept, its heart of gold.

Ruins of a Dream Forgotten

In crumbling stone, the stories fade,
Of castles built, and glories played.
Where laughter once and joy did soar,
Now echoes dwell, forevermore.

Windswept halls, where shadows dwell,
Each corner holds a silent spell.
A garden wild, now overgrown,
Hides secrets in its tangled throne.

The moonlit path, a ghostly trail,
Reveals the heart of this old tale.
In ruin, beauty still remains,
A whisper of forgotten chains.

Lullabies of an Abandoned Kingdom

In twilight's arms, the kingdom sleeps,
Where silence in the night-time creeps.
The castle walls, both proud and tall,
Once echoed with a royal call.

Now cradled deep in shadows' fold,
Their stories lost, yet still so bold.
The lullabies of days gone past,
In gentle winds, they sigh at last.

The air is thick with dreams that weave,
Of love and loss; the heart believes.
An empty throne, a crown of dust,
Reminds us all, in hope we trust.

Gardens of Abandoned Reveries

In gardens where the wildflowers bloom,
Echoes dance in the fading light,
Whispers carry the scent of old perfume,
Dreams forgotten take flight.

Cobwebs weave between the trees,
Secrets linger in the air,
Time stands still with softest breeze,
Memories hanging everywhere.

Pathways crumbled underfoot,
Nature's song begins to fade,
In the shade where silence sits,
Beauty in decay is made.

Every petal tells a tale,
Roots entwined with shadows past,
In this realm where dreams curtail,
Abandoned dreams forever last.

Lost in the Mists of Time

In mists that swirl beneath the moon,
Shadows whisper forgotten sighs,
Haunting echoes of an old tune,
Memories fade where silence lies.

Footsteps trace a winding path,
Through the fog where secrets hide,
Lost moments stir a subtle wrath,
Time drifts like an endless tide.

Ghostly figures in the haze,
Blurred lines of what once was true,
In the labyrinth of lost days,
We search for threads that once we knew.

Yet within the depths of night,
Flickers of hope linger still,
For time, despite its fleeting flight,
Keeps the heart's unbroken will.

The Last Ember of Legacy

In the ashes of what once burned bright,
A flicker remains in the dark,
Stories told in the quiet night,
Whispers of love leave their mark.

Legacies etched in the heart's core,
A warmth that time cannot sear,
Through the shadows, we seek for more,
Each ember recalls those held dear.

Yet the winds carry tales away,
Fading slowly like the sun,
In our silence, we wish to stay,
Guarding the battles lost and won.

For every ember bears a flame,
Each memory holds a song,
In the quiet, we learn their name,
In our hearts, they still belong.

Fractured Mirrors of an Illusory Past

Shattered reflections line the walls,
Images splintered, lost in time,
Echoes linger as silence calls,
Fragments weave an unspoken rhyme.

Each shard holds a story untold,
A glimpse into what might have been,
In the cracks, the past unfolds,
Ghosts of glory, buried within.

Through the labyrinth of fading light,
Whispers cling to the autumn air,
Memory dances, taking flight,
In the twilight, shadows stare.

Yet in the shards, hope glimmers bright,
A mosaic of dreams still to live,
For in each crack, a spark ignites,
In these mirrors, we learn to forgive.

Milton Keynes UK
Ingram Content Group UK Ltd.
UKHW050901161124
451129UK00027B/113

9 789916 901069